Possessing the Promises:

Claiming the Abrahamic Covenant

Morris Cerullo

No part of this book may be reproduced or transmitted in any form or by any means. Electronic or mechanical, including photocopying and recording, or by any information storage or retrieval systems, except as may be expressly permitted in writing.
Requests for permission should be addressed in writing to:

Morris Cerullo World Evangelism
P.O. Box 85277
San Diego, CA 92186

Morris Cerullo World Evangelism of Canada
P.O. Box 3600
Concord, Ontario L4K 1B6

Morris Cerullo World Evangelism of Great Britain
P.O. Box 277, Hemel Hempstead
Herts HP2 7DH England

Copyright © 2010
Morris Cerullo World Evangelism
Printed in the United States of America

Quoted verses of scripture throughout this book may have been taken from any one of the publications below, and we therefore wish to credit them:

The Holy Bible, Authorized King James Version
Used with permission from THE GIDEONS International
1958 Edition, by The National Bible Press, Printed in the USA

The Holy Bible, New King James Version ("NKJV")
Copyright © 1982 and 1994, by Thomas Nelson, Inc., Printed in the USA

The Holy Bible, New International Version ("NIV")
Copyright © 1973, 1978, and 1984, by International Bible Society

The Holy Bible, New American Standard Bible ("NASB")
Copyright © 1960, 1962, 1963, 1968, 1971, 1973, 1975, 1977, 1995
THE LOCKMAN FOUNDATION, A Corporation Not For Profit

The Holy Bible, The Amplified Bible ("AMP")
Copyright © 1954, 1958, 1962, 1964, 1965, 1987 by The Lockman Foundation

The Holy Bible, The Living Bible ("TLB"), Paraphrased
Copyright © 1971, by Tyndale House Publishers, Wheaton, IL 60187

The Holy Bible, The Oxford Annotated Bible,
Revised Standard Version ("RSV")

Copyright © 1962, by Oxford University Press, Inc.,
Division of Christian Education of the National Council of Churches of Christ in the United States of America

All scripture quotations are taken from the Authorized King James Version of the Bible, unless otherwise noted.

All quotations of scripture have been modified with emphasis by the adding of italics. There are places within the quoted scriptures that may have an open quote without a close quote (or vice versa) or an open parenthesis without a close parenthesis (or vice versa) or a word with a capital letter in the middle of a sentence. These are not typographical errors or oversights. They are exact quotes from the versions that we are using.

ACKNOWLEDGEMENT

The author wishes to acknowledge and thank Patricia Hulsey for her tireless efforts on this project. Patricia has worked with Morris Cerullo World Evangelism for almost three decades and has been an invaluable contributor to the work that we do, at home and abroad.

Thank you, Patricia, for your insights, godly spirit,
and substantial pouring out of your time, talents, and prayers.

TABLE OF CONTENTS

INTRODUCTION .... **VII**

Chapter One:
YOU ARE AN HEIR 1

Chapter Two:
THE CUTTING OF COVENANT 9

Chapter Three:
POSSESSING THE PROMISES: PART ONE 21

Chapter Four:
POSSESSING THE PROMISES: PART TWO 33

Chapter Five:
DON'T BE SHUT OUT! 45

Chapter Six:
BLESSED TO BE A BLESSING 51

Appendix:
PERSONALIZED DECLARATIONS OF THE ABRAHAMIC COVENANT 55

PERSONAL JOURNAL 62

INTRODUCTION

Get up. Leave your country, your kindred, and your father's house, God commanded Abraham.

Abraham was an aging man. He was walking alone, beneath the stars, when God spoke to him again. He said: Look now toward heaven, and count the stars, if you are able to number them. I will make of you a great nation, a blessing, the father of many.

Over the years, additional revelations from God and more powerful promises were given to Abraham.

This is a great story, but it is much more than a story. It is more than a historical record of the birth of the nation of Israel. It is more than the story of one man. It is the story of a divine covenant and the supernatural promises of God that He intended to pass from generation to generation, down through the centuries.

What is the true message being conveyed through the story of Abraham and the promises that God gave to him? What is the significance? How do these promises impact believers today? Do they affect your destiny? If so, how? How is your life intricately entwined with the story of this aging patriarch?

CHAPTER ONE

YOU ARE AN HEIR

You are about to discover a spiritual truth that is so tremendous that, when you grasp it, your entire life will change. You are an heir!

You may not have a rich relative or a financial endowment that has been passed down to you, but you are a spiritual heir of an inheritance that is far greater. It is an inheritance that is so great that it encompasses every area of your life. It has the capacity to heal every sickness and painful experience that you have ever passed through, supply every need, and equip you for victorious living and effective service in God's Kingdom. This spiritual inheritance is called *the Abrahamic Covenant.*

The story of Abraham, after whom this covenant is named, begins with his departure from Ur of the Chaldeans in ancient southern Babylonia. Abram (as he was then called) and his family moved north along the trade routes of the ancient world and settled in the prosperous trade center of Haran, several hundred miles to the northwest.

At age 75, while living in Haran, Abram received a call from God to go to an unknown land that the Lord would show him:

> *NOW the Lord had said unto Abram, Get thee out of thy country, and from thy kindred, and from thy father's house, unto a land that I will shew thee: And I will make of thee a great nation, and I will bless thee, and make thy name great; and thou shalt be a blessing: And I will bless them that bless thee, and curse him that curseth thee: and in thee shall all families of the earth be blessed.*
>
> Genesis 12:1-3

God promised Abraham that He would make him and his descendants a great nation. The promise must have seemed unbelievable to Abraham because his wife Sarah was elderly and childless, but Abraham obeyed God and began the long journey into the unknown. (Genesis 11:30-31 and 17:15.)

Abraham traveled south, along the trade routes from Haran, through Shechem and Bethel, to the land of Canaan. This was a populated area, inhabited by the war-like Canaanites, so Abraham's belief that God would ultimately give this land to him and his descendants was a tremendous act of faith:

> *By faith Abraham, when he was called to go out into a place which he should after receive for an inheritance, obeyed; and he went out, not knowing whither he went. By faith he sojourned in the land of promise, as in a strange country, dwelling in tabernacles with Isaac and Jacob, the heirs with him of the same promise: For he looked for a city which hath foundations, whose builder and maker is God.*
>
> Hebrews 11:8-10

CHAPTER ONE: YOU ARE AN HEIR

THE ABRAHAMIC COVENANT

As part of Abraham's calling, and in response to his obedience, God made specific promises. God committed Himself to fulfilling His promises to Abraham. This contractual agreement has been called *the Abrahamic Covenant*. The Bible records several occasions on which God appeared to Abraham to make, confirm, or amend the promises.

The provisions of these agreements—which ultimately would result in blessing all families of the earth—were not only extended to Abraham but to his seed after him, including Isaac, Jacob, and the nation of Israel. Abraham would be the spiritual father of Israel and many other nations:

Neither shall thy name any more be called Abram, but thy name shall be Abraham; for a father of many nations have I made thee.
Genesis 17:5

Though childless at the time, having a barren wife who was well-beyond child-bearing years, Abraham believed these promises from God and acted upon them:

For what saith the scripture? Abraham believed God, and it was counted unto him for righteousness.
Romans 4:3

The Abrahamic Covenant will take you beyond a blessing into the realm of power that makes the impossible possible. As God promised, Abraham was blessed with a son, Isaac, through whom the nation of Israel was birthed:

Through faith also Sara herself received strength to conceive seed, and was delivered of a child when she was past age, because she judged him faithful who had promised. Therefore sprang there even of one, and him as good as dead, so many as the stars of the sky in multitude, and as the sand which is by the sea shore innumerable.

Hebrews 11:11-12

Genesis, Chapters 21-35, records the story of Isaac. As you read through it, you will see the tremendous blessings of God upon his life. The provisions of this covenant then passed to Isaac's son, Jacob.

Despite a rough start, Jacob's life was eventually supernaturally changed. With that internal change, his name was changed from *Jacob* to *Israel*. Jacob was mightily blessed by God through the provisions of the Abrahamic Covenant. He passed these promises to his children, and the nation of Israel was birthed.

THE BLESSING EXTENDS TO YOU

The tremendous blessings of Abraham extend even farther than to the nation of Israel. Apostle Paul declared:

The Spirit itself beareth witness with our spirit, that we are the children of God: And if children, then heirs; heirs of God, and joint-heirs with Christ; if so be that we suffer with him, that we may be also glorified together.

Romans 8:16-17

Romans 4:16 declares that Abraham was the *father of us all*. As you study these blessings of the Abrahamic Covenant, it is important for you to realize that as a child of God, as Abraham's spiritual seed and a joint-heir with Christ, you are an heir to these covenant promises!

Apostle Paul declared: *And if ye be Christ's, then are ye Abraham's seed, and heirs according to the promise* (Galatians 3:29.). This means that being true believers, we are Abraham's spiritual seed.

The promises that God made to Abraham extend through the centuries to us today: *That is, They which are the children of the flesh, these are not the children of God: but the children of the promise are counted for the seed* (Romans 9:8).

As we explore this powerful covenant, you will see that God reveals His plans, purposes, and the blessings that He desires to pour out upon us. Everything we need — spiritually, physically, mentally, and financially — has been provided for us in the Abrahamic Covenant.

Unfortunately, few believers today comprehend this or claim their covenant rights. If we are to receive all that God has provided for us in this powerful covenant, then we must learn its terms, its provisions, and how to take possession of these tremendous blessings.

The purpose of this study is to identify the covenant promises of Abraham and to show you how to claim them as your rightful inheritance. Stop for a moment, and pray, right now, for God to open your spirit to receive this powerful revelation.

AN UNLIMITED BLESSING

This blessing is so great that it extends to areas where the natural mind would say that you were crazy to even have a hope for it. Abraham ... *against hope believed in hope, that he might become the father of many nations, according to that which was spoken, So shall thy seed be* (Romans 4:18).

The Abrahamic Covenant will enable you to believe in hope in the spiritual when there is no hope in the natural:

1. It reaches where the doctor has said there is no hope.
2. It reaches where the banker has said there is no hope.
3. It reaches where the attorney has said there is no hope.
4. It reaches where the marriage counselor has said there is no hope.
5. It reaches where those around you have declared that there is no hope.

Claiming your rights under the Abrahamic Covenant will renew your hope! When Abraham first received this powerful covenant, it was so great that he fell on his face before God (Genesis 17:17.) The Bible declares that Abraham:

> ... *staggered not at the promise of God through unbelief; but was strong in faith, giving glory to God. And being fully persuaded that, what he had promised, he was able also to perform.*
>
> Romans 4:20-21

These promises are so great that they could cause you to stagger or fall on your face spiritually. Like Abraham, however, you must be strong in faith. You must be fully persuaded that the provisions of this covenant are for you and that God is able to bring them to pass in your life.

The Abrahamic Covenant will enable you, by faith, to declare those things that are not as though they are. Abraham called ... *those things which be not as though they were* (Romans 4:17).

This covenant will enable you to speak powerful, prophetic words. Regardless of how circumstances appear in the natural, you will be able to speak healing, salvation, and deliverance, and see miracles manifested in your life.

Like Abraham, to whom God revealed His plans for Sodom, you will receive prophetic revelations and be empowered to intercede in the Spirit. Through your prayers, men and women (like Lot and his family) will be delivered from God's wrath.

Are you ready to receive this tremendous spiritual inheritance?

CHAPTER TWO

THE CUTTING OF COVENANT

The blessings of Abraham, your blessings, are based upon a covenant relationship with God. Before we explore these powerful provisions, it is important for you to understand what a covenant is and the terms upon which your inheritance is based.

A *covenant* is "an agreement between two people that involves promises on the part of each to the other." The Hebrew word for *covenant* is *b'rith*, which means "cutting." Biblically, this refers to a custom in Old Testament times where two people making a covenant passed through the bodies of slain animals after making their agreement.

There Are Actually Six Elements To A Covenant:

1. **Content:** What are the promises being made?
2. **Cause:** For what purpose are these promises being made?
3. **Commitment:** There must be a commitment to the covenant from both the giver and the recipient.
4. **Confirmation:** Both must parties confirm their acceptance of the covenant.
5. **Conflicts:** Conflicts may arise as the covenant is enacted and fulfilled.

6. **Continuum:** The covenant is eternal, perpetual to all generations.

We will observe each of these elements in the Abrahamic Covenant. We will learn the content of the covenant, the cause for which it was given, the commitment of God to the covenant, and the confirmation of its truths as it is fulfilled. We will witness that despite conflicts (such as Abraham's advanced age), the covenant is fulfilled, and its promises passed on to future generations.

The Old Testament contains many examples of people who related to each other through covenants. David and Jonathan entered into a covenant because of their love for each other, an agreement which bound each of them to certain responsibilities. (Read this account in I Samuel 18:3.)

Other examples of covenants between men are both Abraham and Isaac with Abimelech. (Refer to Genesis, Chapters 20 and 26.) Each of their covenants contained these six elements.

CUTTING COVENANT

When a person "cut covenant" in Old Testament times, it involved giving a statement of the terms of the agreement, an oath from each party, a curse upon each if one should break the agreement, and the sealing of the covenant by a blood sacrifice. Violation of such a covenant was considered to be a heinous act.

The truly remarkable thing is that God—Who is holy, omniscient, and omnipotent—consented to entering a covenant with sinful mankind. In the Old Testament, God made a covenant with Abraham and his seed, stated the terms, swore by Himself, and sealed the agreement with

Chapter Two: The Cutting Of Covenant

the blood of sacrificial animals. In the New Testament, this covenant was confirmed through the shedding of the blood of Jesus Christ.

The Greek word for *covenant* that is used in the New Testament means "a contract" or "a will." Simply stated, our covenant with God, based upon the Abrahamic promises, is the title deed to our inheritance. It is a legal, spiritually binding agreement between God and mankind.

When God called Abraham to leave his home and go to the Promised Land, He declared that He would make Abraham a great nation, with many descendants. In Genesis, Chapter 15, Abraham questioned this promise because of his advanced age, and the Lord affirmed it. Abraham's response is a model of believing faith: *And he believed in the* LORD, *and he counted it to him for righteousness* (Genesis 15:6).

Genesis, Chapter 15, describes the ceremony that was commonly used in the ancient world to formalize a covenant. The custom was that the parties making the covenant would walk together between the pieces of slain animals (e.g., Jeremiah 34:18-19). This meant that the terms of the covenant would be mandatory for both parties. If one party became guilty of violating any term of the covenant, it would free the other party from the necessity of fulfilling their own promises.

However, the ceremony that took place in Genesis, Chapter 15, between God and Abraham, confirming the covenant, was different in one very important aspect:

And when the sun was going down, a deep sleep fell upon Abram; And it came to pass, that, when the sun went down, and it was dark, behold a smoking furnace, and a burning lamp that passed between those pieces. In the same day the LORD made a covenant with Abram ... :

Genesis 15:12,17-18

Abraham and God did not walk together between slain animals, as was the custom. God put Abraham in a deep sleep and only God (in the form of a smoking oven and a flaming torch) walked between the pieces of the animals. This meant that the fulfillment of the covenant was based solely upon God's grace, regardless of future failures by Abraham or his descendants.

Abraham could not be responsible for the covenant. He could only be a recipient of the covenant. He might fail, but the covenant would remain intact. God would never fail, for He promised: *My covenant will I not break, nor alter the thing that is gone out of my lips* (Psalms 89:34).

YOU ARE A RECIPIENT

You are a recipient of this powerful covenant, with all of its promised benefits. It has passed to you because you are the spiritual seed of Abraham. No matter how often you fail, no matter how weak you may think you are spiritually, the covenant is not dependent upon you. You are only the recipient. The fulfillment is based solely upon God's grace.

You are a spiritual heir of every blessing of the Abrahamic Covenant. The words *bless* and *blessing* are used repeatedly in these promises. The root word is *barak*. It means "to confer abundant and effective life" and "to endue with power for success, prosperity, and longevity."

The blessings that God conferred upon Abraham—which are passed to us, his spiritual seed—now endue us with the power to experience an abundant, effective life. They assure power for success, prosperity, fruitfulness, healing, blessing, and longevity:

> *The promises were spoken to Abraham and to his seed. The Scripture does not say "and to seeds," meaning many people, but "and to your seed," meaning one person, who is Christ.*
>
> Galatians 3:16, NIV

The blessings of Abraham were given from God through Christ to us. If you are a born-again believer, then these blessings are yours. This is what makes an understanding of the covenant vital today.

Many believers are living far below their spiritual heritage because they do not understand that this covenant extends to them. They do not understand its provisions or how to receive the benefits. This lack of knowledge results in their living defeated and desperate lives. God's Word declares: *My people are destroyed for lack of knowledge: ...* (Hosea 4:6).

The provisions of this covenant are yours. They are passed to you from God through Jesus Christ. The covenant is confirmed in your life the same way that it was confirmed in the life of Abraham.

Jesus Christ walked alone to Calvary. Through His blood-sacrifice, He paid the price for your salvation and the spiritual benefits of this covenant:

> *Now he which stablisheth us with you in Christ, and hath anointed us, is God; Who hath also sealed us, and given the earnest of the Spirit in our hearts.*
>
> II Corinthians 1:21-22

The fulfillment of this covenant is not dependent upon you. It is only dependent upon your obedience. It relies upon your accepting and acting upon the terms of the covenant. You must believe in Jesus Christ, and accept Him as your Savior in order to become the seed of Abraham:

> *But what saith it? The word is nigh thee, even in thy mouth, and in thy heart: that is, the word of faith, which we preach; That if thou shalt confess with thy mouth the Lord Jesus, and shalt believe in thine heart that God hath raised him from the dead, thou shalt be saved. For with the heart man believeth unto righteousness; and with the mouth confession is made unto salvation.*
>
> Romans 10:8-10

The promises of the Abrahamic Covenant are attained by grace, through faith, in the same way that your salvation is secured:

> *For by grace are ye saved through faith; and that not of yourselves: it is the gift of God: Not of works, lest any man should boast.*
>
> Ephesians 2:8-9

THE COVENANT IS BASED ON THE RELATIONSHIP

You cannot enter this covenant without a personal relationship with God. It is not **what** you know about this covenant, its terms, and provisions. It is **Who** you know that will make these blessings a reality in your life.

Chapter Two: The Cutting Of Covenant

God's covenant with Abraham was based on a relationship. Abraham was called "the friend of God":

And the scripture was fulfilled which saith, Abraham believed God, and it was imputed unto him for righteousness: and he was called the Friend of God.

James 2:23

How do you become a friend of God? You accept Jesus Christ as your Savior, and develop a personal relationship with Him through praying, praising, worshiping, reading and studying the Word of God, living by His precepts, and doing His will.

After God gave the powerful promises of this covenant to Abraham, He commanded that the agreement be confirmed by the shedding of blood. Abraham was commanded to circumcise himself and all of the males in his household. This was a sign of the covenant relationship between God and the nation of Israel:

This is my covenant, which ye shall keep, between me and you and thy seed after thee; Every man child among you shall be circumcised. And ye shall circumcise the flesh of your foreskin; and it shall be a token of the covenant betwixt me and you. And he that is eight days old shall be circumcised among you, every man child in your generations, he that is born in the house, or bought with money of any stranger, which is not of thy seed. He that is born in thy house, and he that is bought with thy money, must needs be circumcised: and my covenant shall be in your flesh for an everlasting covenant. And the uncircumcised man child whose flesh of his foreskin is not circumcised, that soul shall be cut off from his people; he hath broken my covenant.

Genesis 17:10-14

During the long journey through the wilderness, the Israelites did not practice circumcision, but it was resumed again before they entered the Promised Land:

> *At that time the LORD said unto Joshua, Make thee sharp knives, and circumcise again the children of Israel the second time. And Joshua made him sharp knives, and circumcised the children of Israel at the hill of the foreskins. And this is the cause why Joshua did circumcise: All the people that came out of Egypt, that were males, even all the men of war, died in the wilderness by the way, after they came out of Egypt. Now all the people that came out were circumcised: but all the people that were born in the wilderness by the way as they came forth out of Egypt, them they had not circumcised. For the children of Israel walked forty years in the wilderness, till all the people that were men of war, which came out of Egypt, were consumed, because they obeyed not the voice of the LORD: unto whom the LORD sware that he would not shew them the land, which the LORD sware unto their fathers that he would give us, a land that floweth with milk and honey. And their children, whom he raised up in their stead, them Joshua circumcised: for they were uncircumcised, because they had not circumcised them by the way. And it came to pass, when they had done circumcising all the people, that they abode in their places in the camp, till they were whole. And the LORD said unto Joshua, This day have I rolled away the reproach of Egypt from off you. Wherefore the name of the place is called Gilgal unto this day.*
>
> Joshua 5:2-9

Israel could not successfully confront the enemy and receive the benefits of the Abrahamic Covenant without the mark of God upon their lives.

SPIRITUAL CIRCUMCISION

The obedient act of circumcising (the cutting of the flesh) was a sign of the Abrahamic Covenant between God and His people. What does circumcision represent to the believer today?

Being people who have been called and ordained by God, desiring to walk in the provisions of the Abrahamic Covenant, we must bear the marks of change upon our lives. Because we are New Testament believers, we no longer circumcise the flesh, but rather our heart is circumcised:

> *In Him also you were circumcised with a circumcision not made with hands, but in a [spiritual] circumcision [performed by] Christ by stripping off the body of the flesh (the whole corrupt, carnal nature with its passions and lusts). [Thus you were circumcised when] you were buried with Him in [your] baptism, in which you were also raised with Him [to a new life] through [your] faith in the working of God [as displayed] when He raised Him up from the dead. And you who were dead in trespasses and in the uncircumcision of your flesh (your sensuality, your sinful carnal nature), [God] brought to life together with [Christ], having [freely] forgiven us all our transgressions, Having cancelled and blotted out and wiped away the handwriting of the note (bond) with its legal decrees and demands which was in force and stood against us (hostile to us). This [note with its regulations, decrees, and demands] He set aside and cleared completely out of our way by nailing it to [His] cross.*
>
> Colossians 2:11-12, AMP

Our circumcision is spiritual, of the heart instead of the flesh, but if you have been circumcised in your heart, there will be external signs, as the men of Israel had visible evidence in their flesh. You will act, talk, and live differently. Your life (your flesh) will bear the marks of change, which are the signs of your covenant relationship with God:

> *For he is not a Jew, which is one outwardly; neither is that circumcision, which is outward in the flesh: But he is a Jew, which is one inwardly; and circumcision is that of the heart, in the spirit, and not in the letter; whose praise is not of men, but of God.*
>
> Romans 2:28-29

The Circumcision Of The Heart Is Two-Fold:

1. **God has a part in it:** *And the LORD thy God will circumcise thine heart* ... (Deuteronomy 30:6).
2. **You have a part in it:** *Circumcise yourselves to the LORD, and take away the foreskins of your heart* ... (Jeremiah 4:4).

You cannot do your part until He does His part. That would simply be a futile attempt at self-improvement. Apostle Paul declared:

> *For we are the circumcision, which worship God in the spirit, and rejoice in Christ Jesus, and have no confidence in the flesh.*
>
> Philippians 3:3

Our spiritual circumcision enables us to enter—by the Spirit, not by the flesh—the covenant blessings of Abraham. The Bible teaches that man is body, soul, and spirit. When you accept Christ as your Savior, the change is spiritual. You experience a spiritual rebirth. (John 3:5-8.) Your spirit, not your flesh, is born again.

CHAPTER TWO: THE CUTTING OF COVENANT

After your new spiritual birth, your soul (your mind, will, and emotions) must be supernaturally changed in order to live out this new life. For years, your soul has ruled your spirit and your flesh. Whatever you desired, you did, whether it was drugs, alcohol, pornography, sexual immorality, etc. You did not exercise control over emotions, such as anger, unforgiveness, and bitterness. You went where you wanted to go and did what you wanted to do.

Repetition of sinful behavior leads to more of the same, until certain actions are so entrenched in our lives that we cannot stop. We become enslaved to habitual sin, and spiritual strongholds are erected. This is what Apostle Paul struggled with after his conversion. He described this struggle in Romans 7:15-21.

You cannot change your soulish nature on your own. Self-effort will not rid you of habitual sin; Paul found that out. Addictions typically cannot be broken through self-effort. You must let God supernaturally change your soulish realm — your mind, will, and emotions. For years, your sinful, soulish nature has controlled your body and spirit. Now you must learn to let your redeemed spirit control your body and soul.

The covenant promises that were made with Abraham are not for everyone. They are only for those who have entered the blood covenant with Jesus Christ by accepting His sacrifice for their sin. It is for those who have circumcised their flesh and bear the marks of change upon their lives. It is for those who obey God's directive to claim the promises by faith.

Do not be afraid of the "knife" of God's Word as it marks your life. The reproach of Egypt (sin) must be rolled away. You must put off the filth of the flesh. As you camp in the very shadow of your enemies, as Israel did, you must realize that you cannot possess these promises by the power of the flesh. You must disable your flesh, and trust solely in the power of Almighty God. The promises of this covenant will be possessed only by the weakness of the flesh and by the power of the Spirit.

Now that we have established the spiritual foundations of this tremendous revelation, how it was given, and how to receive it, we will explore the provisions of this agreement between God and His people.

The Abrahamic Covenant is comprised of amazing, powerful promises that will change your life forever!

CHAPTER THREE

POSSESSING THE PROMISES

PART ONE

In this chapter and in Chapter Four, we will identify each biblical reference to the Abrahamic Covenant, list its provisions, and explain what they mean to believers today.

The Abrahamic Covenant is an unconditional covenant. This means that God's promises are without qualification. Fulfillment is dependent upon God, not man. While enjoyment of the blessings of the covenant may be conditional upon obedience, the fulfillment of the promises is not. For example, ownership of the land that God promised Abraham was unconditional. The enjoyment of the land, however, was conditional upon Abraham's obedience to enter it and possess it.

When God confirmed this covenant, He said: *I swear.* This is strong language. God swore by Himself that the promises He had made to Abraham and his seed would be fulfilled. Nothing will stop God from fulfilling this covenant in your life:

For when God made [His] promise to Abraham, He swore by Himself, since He had no one greater by whom to swear, Saying, Blessing I certainly will bless you and multiplying I will multiply you. [Gen. 22:16, 17.] And so it was that he [Abraham], having waited long and endured patiently, realized and obtained [in the birth of Isaac as a pledge of what was to come] what God had promised him. Men indeed swear by a greater [than themselves], and with them in all disputes the oath taken for confirmation is final [ending strife]. Accordingly God also, in His desire to show more convincingly and beyond doubt to those who were to inherit the promise the unchangeableness of His purpose and plan, intervened (mediated) with an oath. This was so that, by two unchangeable things [His promise and His oath] in which it is impossible for God ever to prove false or deceive us, we who have fled [to Him] for refuge might have mighty indwelling strength and strong encouragement to grasp and hold fast the hope appointed for us and set before [us]. [Now] we have this [hope] as a sure and steadfast anchor of the soul [it cannot slip and it cannot break down under whoever steps out upon it – a hope] that reaches farther and enters into [the very certainty of the Presence] within the veil, [Lev. 16:2.]

Hebrews 6:13-19, AMP

God swore by Himself so that we could function from a position of knowing and be convinced beyond any doubt. God has promised: *My covenant will I not break, nor alter the thing that is gone out of my lips* (Psalms 89:34).

As you study these powerful provisions, remember what you learned in previous chapters. Every promise is yours to claim. You are a spiritual heir of these powerful proclamations.

Genesis 12:1-3,7:

1 *NOW the LORD had said unto Abram, Get thee out of thy country, and from thy kindred, and from thy father's house, unto a land that I will shew thee:*

Chapter Three: Possessing The Promises: Part One

2 And I will make of thee a great nation, and I will bless thee, and make thy name great; and thou shalt be a blessing:

3 And I will bless them that bless thee, and curse him that curseth thee: and in thee shall all families of the earth be blessed.

7 And the LORD appeared unto Abram, and said, Unto thy seed will I give this land: and there builded he an altar unto the LORD, who appeared unto him.

In this passage, God promised Abraham that He would give him a land, make him a great nation, make his name great, bless him, and make him a blessing to others. God also promised to bless those who blessed him and curse those who cursed him.

How does this apply to your life? God has a spiritual land, a divine destiny, for you. He has a specific plan for your life, an expected end:

For I know the thoughts that I think toward you, saith the LORD, thoughts of peace, and not of evil, to give you an expected end.

Jeremiah 29:11

God wants to bless you so that through you, the nations (families) of the earth will be blessed. You are blessed in order to be a blessing.

God has promised to bless those who bless you and curse those who curse you. When people rise up against you, you won't need to defend yourself. God will deal with your enemies because you are walking in the provisions of this covenant. You won't have to fight. You won't have to struggle.

Genesis 13:15-17:

15 *For all the land which thou seest, to thee will I give it, and to thy seed for ever.*

16 *And I will make thy seed as the dust of the earth: so that if a man can number the dust of the earth, then shall thy seed also be numbered.*

17 *Arise, walk through the land in the length of it and in the breadth of it; for I will give it unto thee.*

In this passage, God promised Abraham that the land—his inheritance from God—would be his forever and that he would pass this blessing to his seed. While this has a specific application to the nation of Israel, it also applies to believers today. The inheritance that God has given to you is eternal, without end. There are no exclusions. There are no disclaimers. You can receive this blessing and pass it to your children and your spiritual seed forever.

God also promised Abraham that his seed would be as the dust of the earth. Even if you are barren and without natural children, God wants to birth from you a spiritual seed that will reproduce throughout the nations. God declares over you:

> *SING, O barren, thou that didst not bear; break forth into singing, and cry aloud, thou that didst not travail with child: for more are the children of the desolate than the children of the married wife, saith the* Lord. *Enlarge the place of thy tent, and let them stretch forth the curtains of thine habitations: spare not, lengthen thy cords, and strengthen thy stakes; For thou shalt break forth on the right hand and on the left; and thy seed shall inherit the Gentiles, and make the desolate cities to be inhabited.*
>
> Isaiah 54:1-3

Chapter Three: Possessing The Promises: Part One

When you embrace the provisions of this covenant, you will need to enlarge your borders. You must put aside small thinking because the blessing that God is about to pour upon you will not fit within the parameters of your natural reasoning. It will not be poured into the old vessels of tradition. It will not be limited. You will break forth on the right hand and on the left. You will inherit the Gentiles (the nations). You will march into the desolation of sinful cities, violent slums, dangerous prisons, and drug houses to deliver people from the very gates of hell.

God commanded Abraham to walk through the land and declared that He would give it to him. Applied to us spiritually, this means that we can walk through the land of our households, and claim our children for God. We can walk through the desolation of our cities and nations and know that God has given this spiritual territory into our hands.

Rise up today in the spirit world. Walk through the land of your household, your ministry, your community, and your nation. Being an heir of the Abrahamic Covenant, God has declared: I will give it unto you!

Genesis 15:1-21:

> 1 *AFTER these things the word of the LORD came unto Abram in a vision, saying, Fear not, Abram: I am thy shield, and thy exceeding great reward.*
>
> 2 *And Abram said, Lord GOD, what wilt thou give me, seeing I go childless, and the steward of my house is this Eliezer of Damascus?*
>
> 3 *And Abram said, Behold, to me thou hast given no seed: and, lo, one born in my house is mine heir.*

4 And, behold, the word of the LORD came unto him, saying, This shall not be thine heir; but he that shall come forth out of thine own bowels shall be thine heir.

5 And he brought him forth abroad, and said, Look now toward heaven, and tell the stars, if thou be able to number them: and he said unto him, So shall thy seed be.

6 And he believed in the LORD; and he counted it to him for righteousness.

7 And he said unto him, I am the LORD that brought thee out of Ur of the Chaldees, to give thee this land to inherit it.

8 And he said, Lord GOD, whereby shall I know that I shall inherit it?

9 And he said unto him, Take me an heifer of three years old, and a she goat of three years old, and a ram of three years old, and a turtledove, and a young pigeon.

10 And he took unto him all these, and divided them in the midst, and laid each piece one against another: but the birds divided he not.

11 And when the fowls came down upon the carcases, Abram drove them away.

12 And when the sun was going down, a deep sleep fell upon Abram; and, lo, an horror of great darkness fell upon him.

13 And he said unto Abram, Know of a surety that thy seed shall be a stranger in a land that is not theirs, and shall serve them; and they shall afflict them four hundred years;

Chapter Three: Possessing The Promises: Part One

14 *And also that nation, whom they shall serve, will I judge: and afterward shall they come out with great substance.*

15 *And thou shalt go to thy fathers in peace; thou shalt be buried in a good old age.*

16 *But in the fourth generation they shall come hither again: for the iniquity of the Amorites is not yet full.*

17 *And it came to pass, that, when the sun went down, and it was dark, behold a smoking furnace, and a burning lamp that passed between those pieces.*

18 *In the same day the LORD made a covenant with Abram, saying, Unto thy seed have I given this land, from the river of Egypt unto the great river, the river Euphrates:*

19 *The Kenites, and the Kenizzites, and the Kadmonites,*

20 *And the Hittites, and the Perizzites, and the Rephaims,*

21 *And the Amorites, and the Canaanites, and the Girgashites, and the Jebusites.*

In this passage, God declared to Abraham: I am thy shield. This is one of the most powerful declarations of the covenant: God is our shield!

This shield is our salvation: *Thou hast also given me the shield of thy salvation ...* (Psalms 18:35).

This shield lifts us up from despondency and discouragement: *But thou, O LORD, art a shield for me; my glory, and the lifter up of mine head* (Psalms 3:3).

This shield compasses us with favor: *For thou, LORD, wilt bless the righteous; with favour wilt thou compass him as with a shield* (Psalms 5:12).

This shield is our strength and joy: *The LORD is my strength and my shield; my heart trusted in him, and I am helped: therefore my heart greatly rejoiceth; and with my song will I praise him* (Psalms 28:7).

This shield is our help in every situation: *Our soul waiteth for the LORD: he is our help and our shield* (Psalms 33:20).

This shield provides grace, glory, and all good things: *For the LORD God is a sun and shield: the LORD will give grace and glory: no good thing will he withhold from them that walk uprightly* (Psalms 84:11).

This shield of truth is our protection: *He shall cover thee with his feathers, and under his wings shalt thou trust: his truth shall be thy shield and buckler. Thou shalt not be afraid for the terror by night; nor for the arrow that flieth by day; Nor for the pestilence that walketh in darkness; nor for the destruction that wasteth at noonday. A thousand shall fall at thy side, and ten thousand at thy right hand; but it shall not come nigh thee* (Psalms 91:4-7).

This shield of faith enables us to stop the enemy in his tracks: *Above all, taking the shield of faith, wherewith ye shall be able to quench all the fiery darts of the wicked* (Ephesians 6:16).

This one promise—I am thy shield—encompasses every need in your life. It lifts you from the despondency of painful experiences. This shield protects you from evil and enables you to stop the enemy in his tracks. It provides salvation, faith, strength, and joy. You don't have to struggle for these things. They are yours because God is your shield.

God also told Abraham, I am thy exceeding great reward. This promise includes both spiritual and material blessings. Abraham was not only blessed spiritually by his relationship

CHAPTER THREE: POSSESSING THE PROMISES: PART ONE

with God and through his ministry to the nations, but he was also blessed materially. He possessed great wealth, as did his immediate heirs Isaac and Jacob.

God blessed Abraham materially because He knew that he would honor Him with the tithe. (Genesis 14:18-20.) God knew that Abraham would use his wealth wisely for the extension of heaven's purposes.

God wants to bless you with both spiritual and material rewards. God is the One Who gives you the power to get wealth and declares:

But thou shalt remember the LORD thy God: for it is he that giveth thee power to get wealth, that he may establish his covenant which he sware unto thy fathers, as it is this day.
Deuteronomy 8:18

The power to get wealth is a part of the Abrahamic Covenant. God gives you the power to get what you need for yourself, your family, and your ministry. Cast aside a welfare mentality. Rebuke all negative thinking regarding your finances. Make this covenant declaration today: He gives ME the power to get wealth so that He can establish with ME the covenant He made with Abraham!

Remember that God blessed Abraham because He knew that Abraham would use his resources wisely to extend heaven's purposes. If you will put the Kingdom of God first in your finances, you will be blessed:

But seek ye first the kingdom of God, and his righteousness; and all these things shall be added unto you.
Matthew 6:33

The financial blessings of the Abrahamic Covenant are released when you give of your resources to God:

> *Will a man rob God? Yet ye have robbed me. But ye say, Wherein have we robbed thee? In tithes and offerings. Ye are cursed with a curse: for ye have robbed me, even this whole nation. Bring ye all the tithes into the storehouse, that there may be meat in mine house, and prove me now herewith, saith the LORD of hosts, if I will not open you the windows of heaven, and pour you out a blessing, that there shall not be room enough to receive it. And I will rebuke the devourer for your sakes, and he shall not destroy the fruits of your ground; neither shall your vine cast her fruit before the time in the field, saith the LORD of hosts. And all nations shall call you blessed: for ye shall be a delightsome land, saith the LORD of hosts.*
>
> Malachi 3:8-12

Do you want to be under a curse or a blessing? This passage is very clear as to how to enter into the Abrahamic Covenant.

There is a negative aspect to the covenant that is revealed in this passage. God delivered the prophetic Word that Abraham's seed would be in bondage, but He also promised that He would bring them out with great substance (Genesis 15:13-14). God confirmed that Abraham's seed would inherit the Promised Land, their destiny. God set Abraham's boundaries. None of the wars in and around Israel have changed these parameters. It belongs to them FOREVER!

God has brought you out of sin, shame, and bondage to bring you into your God-ordained destiny. None of the battles that you will face will change the promises that God has

CHAPTER THREE: POSSESSING THE PROMISES: PART ONE

made. Your promised land—your divine destiny—is yours FOREVER! All that you must do is claim it!

Have you experienced a bondage? Have you been held captive by the bondage of sin, abuse, or addiction? God's Word to you today is that it is time to come out from its grip. You will not only come out of it, but you will come out with great victory and substance. God will use the difficulties, the pain, the abuse, and the rejection that you have experienced to touch the lives of multitudes. Every difficulty in your life has simply set you on a course to fulfill your destiny.

In this passage, God also promised Abraham: *And thou shalt go to thy fathers in peace; thou shalt be buried in a good old age* (Genesis 15:15). He promised Abraham a long life, followed by eternal life with his ancestors who had passed away.

God is not promising that we all will live as long as Abraham lived, but He is declaring that we will live to a good old age. You may ask: But what about those who die young? When we live under the Abrahamic Covenant, we will live long enough to fulfill our God-given destiny. For some, that will be sooner than others.

For example, the five missionaries who were martyred by the Auca Indians in Ecuador years ago were young in terms of chronological age, but these men lived long enough to fulfill their destinies. Even today, their legacy lives on through books and films, like *Through Gates Of Splendor* and *The End Of The Spear*. The story of their sacrifice has resulted in multitudes responding to the call of God to the mission field over the years.

In this provision, God also guarantees eternal life. In the end, we will be gathered to our fathers, the saints of God who have preceded us in death:

But I would not have you to be ignorant, brethren, concerning them which are asleep, that ye sorrow not, even as others which have no hope. For if we believe that Jesus died and rose again, even so them also which sleep in Jesus will God bring with him. For this we say unto you by the word of the Lord, that we which are alive and remain unto the coming of the Lord shall not prevent them which are asleep. For the Lord himself shall descend from heaven with a shout, with the voice of the archangel, and with the trump of God: and the dead in Christ shall rise first: Then we which are alive and remain shall be caught up together with them in the clouds to meet the Lord in the air: and so shall we ever be with the Lord. Wherefore comfort one another with these words.

I Thessalonians 4:13-18

God declared again in Genesis, Chapter 15, that from Abraham's own body would come an heir and that his descendants would multiply as the stars of heaven. We will learn more about this in the next chapter.

What tremendous promises, and we are not even halfway through! I encourage you to believe the Word of the Lord that is coming to you through the pages of this book. Accept these covenant promises! Begin right now, today, to take possession of every word of this divine revelation.

We have even more powerful promises to claim. Are you ready to continue?

CHAPTER FOUR

POSSESSING THE PROMISES

PART TWO

We are only about halfway finished with identifying the blessings of Abraham. Are you ready to receive the remainder of this revelation? Let us resume our spiritual adventure and continue to embrace the provisions of our divine inheritance.

Genesis 17:1-22:

1 *AND when Abram was ninety years old and nine, the LORD appeared to Abram, and said unto him, I am the Almighty God; walk before me, and be thou perfect.*

2 *And I will make my covenant between me and thee, and will multiply thee exceedingly.*

3 *And Abram fell on his face: and God talked with him, saying,*

4 *As for me, behold, my covenant is with thee, and thou shalt be a father of many nations.*

5 *Neither shall thy name any more be called Abram, but thy name shall be Abraham; for a father of many nations have I made thee.*

6 *And I will make thee exceeding fruitful, and I will make nations of thee, and kings shall come out of thee.*

7 And I will establish my covenant between me and thee and thy seed after thee in their generations for an everlasting covenant, to be a God unto thee, and to thy seed after thee.

8 And I will give unto thee, and to thy seed after thee, the land wherein stranger, all the land of Canaan, for an everlasting possession; and I will be their God.

9 And God said unto Abraham, Thou shalt keep my covenant therefore, thou, and thy seed after thee in their generations.

10 This is my covenant, which ye shall keep, between me and you and thy seed after thee; Every man child among you shall be circumcised.

11 And ye shall circumcise the flesh of your foreskin; and it shall be a token of the covenant betwixt me and you.

12 And he that is eight days old shall be circumcised among you, every man child in your generations, he that is born in the house, or bought with money of any stranger, which is not of thy seed.

13 He that is born in thy house, and he that is bought with thy money, must needs be circumcised: and my covenant shall be in your flesh for an everlasting covenant.

14 And the uncircumcised man child whose flesh of his foreskin is not circumcised, that soul shall be cut off from his people; he hath broken my covenant.

15 And God said unto Abraham, As for Sarai thy wife, thou shalt not call her name Sarai, but Sarah shall her name be.

16 And I will bless her, and give thee a son also of her: yea, I will bless her, and she shall be a mother of nations; kings of people shall be of her.

Chapter Four: Possessing The Promises: Part Two

17 Then Abraham fell upon his face, and laughed, and said in his heart, Shall a child be born unto him that is an hundred years old? and shall Sarah, that is ninety years old, bear?

18 And Abraham said unto God, O that Ishmael might live before thee!

19 And God said, Sarah thy wife shall bear thee a son indeed; and thou shalt call his name Isaac: and I will establish my covenant with him for an everlasting covenant, and with his seed after him.

20 And as for Ishmael, I have heard thee: Behold, I have blessed him, and will make him fruitful, and will multiply him exceedingly; twelve princes shall he beget, and I will make him a great nation.

21 But my covenant will I establish with Isaac, which Sarah shall bear unto thee at this set time in the next year.

22 And he left off talking with him, and God went up from Abraham.

In this revelation, God promised Abraham that his seed would be multiplied, that he would be exceedingly fruitful, and that he would be a father of nations. God changed his name from *Abram* to *Abraham*, meaning "father of a great multitude." God changed Sarai's name to *Sarah*, meaning "princess of a multitude." Often, in Bible times, names were changed to reflect a changed nature. This was true in Old Testament times when God changed Jacob's name to Israel and in New Testament times when Saul's name was changed to *Paul*.

How do these name-change promises apply to you spiritually? God wants to take your old sin nature, your past and your failures, and make everything new:

> *Therefore if any man be in Christ, he is a new creature: old things are passed away; behold, all things are become new.*
> II Corinthians 5:17

The new name that God wants to give you will attract the Gentiles (the nations) because they will see the difference in your life:

> *And the Gentiles shall see thy righteousness, and all kings thy glory: and thou shalt be called by a new name, which the mouth of the LORD shall name.*
> Isaiah 62:2

What is the new name by which we will be called? It is God's Name:

> *Him that overcometh will I make a pillar in the temple of my God, and he shall go no more out: and I will write upon him the name of my God, and the name of the city of my God, which is new Jerusalem, which cometh down out of heaven from my God: and I will write upon him my new name.*
> Revelation 3:12

God's Name rests upon you. You are called a *Christian: ... And the disciples were called Christians first in Antioch* (Acts 11:26). You are no longer the servant of sin. You have a new name. You bear the Name of Jesus Christ upon your life. Walk worthy of that Name! Paul admonishes us to: *... walk worthy of God, who hath called you unto his kingdom and glory* (I Thessalonians 2:12).

Much of this passage regarding the covenant deals with Ishmael and Isaac. While this has immediate and future fulfillment in Israel and other nations, there are also spiritual applications.

Chapter Four: Possessing The Promises: Part Two

For example, God promised Abraham that Sarah, who was beyond child-bearing years, would bear a son. This was an unnatural, outrageous promise. The blessing of Abraham includes outrageous promises. We need to believe God for the impossible, for the outrageous!

God told Abraham that from his own loins would come a son with whom the covenant would be established. While God would bless Ishmael and make a great nation of him, it was Isaac and his seed who would receive the covenant promises. How does this part of the covenant apply to us spiritually? Let's trace the story.

Initially, after receiving the promise of a son, Abraham tried to bring forth this covenant blessing through self-effort. Ishmael was consequently born of a servant girl named *Hagar*. Abraham knew that God wanted to make him the father of a great nation, but it seemed impossible that an heir could come through Sarah, his elderly and barren wife.

So, he took matters into his own hands, and Ishmael was born. Whose power was behind Ishmael's birth? That of Abraham or that of God? Was the attempted fulfillment of the promised blessing man-made or God-made? Was it birthed of the flesh or of the Spirit? Ishmael represents your human attempts to achieve God's blessings. You can bring an Ishmael on the scene any time through your own efforts.

Who is the source of your blessings? Who is the source of your spiritual vision? Who is the source of your ministry? Is it a useless striving of the flesh to attain, or is it being birthed by the Spirit of God?

When asked: *... What shall we do, that we might work the works of God?* (John 6:28), Jesus responded: *... This is the work of God ...* (John 6:29). By saying this, He was indicating that He, Himself, was the Source for being able to work the works of God. God did not want Ishmael (representing the efforts of the flesh) to be the source of the blessing. God Himself was the Source.

God is the Source of these tremendous blessings that we are studying. You cannot bring them forth in your life through self-effort. Remember what we learned about the cutting of this covenant? God passed through the sacrifice alone. The fulfillment of these promises is not based on your self-effort. You are simply a recipient.

It is time for Isaac to be birthed in your spirit. In order for this to happen, Ishmael (the flesh) must be cast out. God told Abraham that Isaac, the son of the Spirit, could not abide in the same house with Ishmael, the son of the flesh.

God is saying to you, as He did to Abraham when Ishmael was cast out: *Grieve not for Ishmael* [self-effort], *for in Isaac shall your seed be called.* The blessing comes by the Spirit, not by the flesh. Put aside all of your self-effort, your plans, your ambitions, and your preconceived ideas.

Paul compared the Old Covenant to Ishmael because it was dependent upon the flesh. He compared the New Covenant to Isaac because it is based upon faith and the quickening power of the Holy Spirit:

For it is written, that Abraham had two sons, the one by a bondmaid, the other by a freewoman. But he who was of the bondwoman was born after the flesh; but he of the freewoman was by promise. Which things are an allegory: for these are the two covenants; ... . Now we, brethren, as Isaac was,

Chapter Four: Possessing The Promises: Part Two

are the children of promise. So then, brethren, we are not children of the bondwoman, but of the free.
Galatians 4:22-24,28,31

God told Abraham that his promised seed would come through Isaac. We are children of promise because we are of the spiritual seed of Isaac, birthed by the Spirit and not by the flesh.

In Genesis 17:8, God also gave Abraham the title deed to the land of Israel forever. While there is an evident prophetic meaning in this promise to Israel, there is also a spiritual application to us.

In Genesis 13:17, God commanded Abraham to: *Arise, walk through the land in the length of it and in the breadth of it; for I will give it unto thee.* How does this apply to believers today? God is saying to us: Don't limit Me! Get up! Walk through your spiritual inheritance, the length and breadth of it! I have given it to you!

One of the most powerful declarations in this passage is that the covenant was established between God, Abraham, and his seed to be an everlasting covenant:

And I will establish my covenant between me and thee and thy seed after thee in their generations for an everlasting covenant, to be a God unto thee, and to thy seed after thee.
Genesis 17:7

God declared that He would ... *be a God unto thee, and unto thy seed after thee.* Is He your God? Do you accept this part of the verse? Then you can also accept the remainder of the passage which declares that the blessings of Abraham will be passed to future generations—that includes you! You are the seed of Abraham!

POSSESSING THE PROMISES: Claiming The Abrahamic Covenant

This is an everlasting covenant. It didn't cease with the death of Abraham. It didn't cease with the death of Isaac. It was not voided when Jacob passed away. In fact, it was confirmed to us through the blood of Jesus Christ on Calvary. It is an eternal covenant!

Genesis 22:16-18:

16 *And said, By myself have I sworn, saith the* LORD, *for because thou hast done this thing, and hast not withheld thy son, thine only son:*

17 *That in blessing I will bless thee, and in multiplying I will multiply thy seed as the stars of the heaven, and as the sand which is upon the sea shore; and thy seed shall possess the gate of his enemies;*

18 *And in thy seed shall all the nations of the earth be blessed; because thou hast obeyed my voice.*

In this passage, God confirmed again to Abraham—and through it, He also declares to us today—His desire to bless him (us). We will experience a supernatural multiplication of our spiritual seed, and our seed will possess the gates of the enemy and bless the nations of the earth.

In *The Elijah Institute* and by raising up God's Victorious Army, we are passing the spiritual mantle of the anointing to thousands of men and women around the world, who are willing to forsake everything for the sake of God's call. We are experiencing a supernatural multiplication of our spiritual seed.

The men and women we are raising up are not weak, anemic believers. They are not people who must be nursed along and coddled spiritually. They are spiritual warriors

CHAPTER FOUR: POSSESSING THE PROMISES: PART TWO

who are possessing the gates of the enemy and blessing the nations. They are walking in the promises of the Abrahamic Covenant.

This is what God wants to do through you, your life, and your ministry. Fathers and mothers, claim this for your children. Pastors, claim this for your church members. Ministers, claim this for your followers. Teachers, declare this over your students. Your seed will multiply. You will possess the gates of the enemy and bless the nations of the earth.

God sealed all of the provisions of this divine covenant. He guaranteed these promises with His own oath, saying: *... By myself have I sworn ...* (Genesis 22:16).

Referring to God's covenant promises, Apostle Paul declared:

For men verily swear by the greater: and an oath for confirmation is to them an end of all strife. Wherein God, willing more abundantly to shew unto the heirs of promise the immutability of his counsel, confirmed it by an oath: That by two immutable things, in which it was impossible for God to lie, we might have a strong consolation, who have fled for refuge to lay hold upon the hope set before us: Which hope we have as an anchor of the soul, both sure and stedfast, and which entereth into that within the vail;
Hebrews 6:16-19

There are two undeniable proofs that guarantee the fulfillment of every promise that God has made:

For when God made promise to Abraham, because he could swear by no greater, he sware by himself, Saying, Surely blessing I will bless thee, and multiplying I will multiply

thee. And so, after he had patiently endured, he obtained the promise. For men verily swear by the greater: and an oath for confirmation is to them an end of all strife.
Hebrews 6:13-16

First, God swears by Himself. There is no one greater than God, and God swore by Himself that this covenant would be fulfilled. He put everything He is on the line: His holiness, righteousness, power, integrity, mercy, etc. He swore by all that He is and declared: ... *By myself I have sworn* ... (Genesis 22:16). The promises of this covenant are secure and sealed because they are made on the basis of God Himself.

Second, He seals these promises with an oath. You can trust God's promises because they are sealed by His sacred oath. He swears by it, and He does not lie. It is impossible for God to lie:

God is not a man, that he should lie; neither the son of man, that he should repent: hath he said, and shall he not do it? or hath he spoken, and shall he not make it good?
Numbers 23:19

So shall my word be that goeth forth out of my mouth: it shall not return unto me void, but it shall accomplish that which I please, and it shall prosper in the thing whereto I sent it.
Isaiah 55:11

God provided these two *immutable* proofs to end all doubt, fear, and uncertainty. They provide a sure and steadfast anchor for your soul, no matter what your circumstances, problems, or challenges.

Chapter Four: Possessing The Promises: Part Two

Synonyms for the word *immutable* are: abiding, changeless, consistent, constant, enduring, ceaseless, continual, endless, permanent, stable, unchanging, unalterable, and eternal. Is that secure enough for you?

Make this declaration right now: God has sworn by Himself and sealed His Word with an oath. His promises to me will be fulfilled.

CHAPTER FIVE

DON'T BE SHUT OUT!

*O*utrageous! Impossible! Amazing! These are the only terms that can describe the covenant promises of Abraham that we have examined, and they are all yours through Jesus Christ! Remember that, as an heir in the natural world must lay claim to their inheritance, these tremendous promises are only yours if you take possession of them.

This chapter will examine two powerful, spiritual forces that will attempt to shut you out of the promises of God: unbelief and fear.

UNBELIEF WILL SHUT YOU OUT

At Kadesh-Barnea, God directed Israel to advance and take possession of the land that was promised through the Abrahamic Covenant. When they heard the negative report of ten of the twelve spies, their hearts were filled with unbelief:

And Caleb stilled the people before Moses, and said, Let us go up at once, and possess it; for we are well able to overcome it. But the men that went up with him said, We be not able to go up against the people; for they are stronger than we.

POSSESSING THE PROMISES: Claiming The Abrahamic Covenant

> *And they brought up an evil report of the land which they had searched unto the children of Israel, saying, The land, through which we have gone to search it, is a land that eateth up the inhabitants thereof; and all the people that we saw in it are men of a great stature. And there we saw the giants, the sons of Anak, which come of the giants: and we were in our own sight as grasshoppers, and so we were in their sight.*
>
> Numbers 13:30-33

The Israelites refused to believe the faith-filled reports of Caleb and Joshua. They instead listened to the negative reports of the other spies, which shattered their faith. They did not believe that they could conquer the land. They refused to believe the promises of God. Hebrews 3:19 declares that *... they could not enter in because of unbelief.*

Why are the promises of the Abrahamic Covenant not being manifested in the lives of many believers? Because of unbelief. They don't believe that these promises are for them. We have studied the tremendous promises that were given to Abraham and learned how they are passed down to us, but if we do not believe and act upon this revelation, we will fail to receive it. Unbelief shut an entire generation out of the Promised Land, and it will prevent you from taking possession of these promises. Unbelief shuts off the supernatural life-flow of God.

One of the saddest examples of people being shut off from experiencing the mighty manifestation of God's promises is found in The Gospel According to Saint Mark. Jesus did mighty miracles throughout Galilee. He healed the sick and raised the dead. He opened blind eyes and cast out demons. Yet, when Jesus came to Nazareth, He could do no mighty works there:

CHAPTER FIVE: DON'T BE SHUT OUT

And he could there do no mighty work, save that he laid his hands upon a few sick folk, and healed them. And he marvelled because of their unbelief... .

Mark 6:5-6

Jesus was not limited because His power was not limited. His power had not changed. The only thing that prevented these people from receiving the blessings of God was their unbelief. Instead of being shut out of these promises by unbelief, you must shut unbelief out. Don't allow unbelief to enter your mind. Whatever God says, believe it!

Make this declaration: I won't let unbelief limit God's work in my life or hinder me from receiving these promises. I won't be shut out!

FEAR WILL SHUT YOU OUT

The other powerful, spiritual force that will shut you out of God's promises is fear. The Israelites did not enter the Promised Land because of their fear. When they heard the negative reports of the spies, they developed a "grasshopper mentality," which kept them out of the Promised Land. They saw the enemy as being a giant and themselves as being grasshoppers in comparison. They were afraid to enter the land to claim their rightful possessions. (Numbers 13:33.)

One of the first things that God said to Abraham when sharing the provisions of this covenant with him was: *... Fear not ...* (Genesis 15:1). God knew that these promises were so great that Abraham might fear at their very magnitude.

Fear is a demon spirit that Satan uses to torment, control, dominate, oppress, and bind Christians. Paul told Timothy:

For God hath not given us the spirit of fear; but of power, and of love, and of a sound mind (II Timothy 1:7). Psalmist David declared:

> *Though an host should encamp against me, my heart shall not fear: though war should rise against me, in this will I be confident. One thing have I desired of the LORD, that will I seek after; that I may dwell in the house of the LORD all the days of my life, to behold the beauty of the LORD, and to enquire in his temple.*
>
> Psalms 27:3-4

David was determined that fear would not keep him from entering the Presence of God or from claiming all that God had for him.

Make this declaration: I reject the spirit of fear. God has not given it to me, so I know where it came from! I will not be shut out of the promises of God because of fear!

IT IS TIME TO COME OUT OF THE WILDERNESS

Through fear and unbelief, Israel had initially failed to take possession of their inheritance. They forfeited their covenant promises and wandered in the wilderness for forty long years.

Likewise, for years, the Church has been wandering in a spiritual wilderness. Like Israel, because of fear and unbelief they have failed to take possession of their rightful inheritance. This is exactly where many believers are today. They have entered the blood-covenant relationship with God, as Israel did during the Passover in Egypt, but they have not taken possession of their inheritance.

Chapter Five: Don't Be Shut Out

Many believers have not realized that these covenant promises belong to them. Not knowing what is legally theirs, they have forfeited their covenant rights and privileges simply because they did not claim them.

What about you? Like the children of Israel, have you wandered in a spiritual wilderness and failed to take possession of your inheritance?

No more! Through the pages of this study, you are learning what is rightfully yours. It is time to come out of the wilderness, and claim your rightful inheritance.

You do not have to struggle to receive these promises. You do not have to wrestle to receive them. Jacob was an heir to the covenant promises of Abraham, but he did not realize the truth of his position in God, so he struggled for years. He did not enjoy the provisions that had already been given to him. He manipulated and deceived others to obtain what he wanted.

Faith is a fact, but faith is also an act. What Jacob needed to do (and what we, believers, need to do) is to realize who we are in God, and act upon that knowledge. We are heirs of the promises!

When Jacob finally came to the realization of who he was in God and the promises that he had inherited, not only was his life changed, but his name was also changed. If you would know yourself as you are known by God, then you would realize that not only has He created and redeemed you, but He has also endowed you with all of the tremendous promises of the Abrahamic Covenant.

Stop struggling! Stop running, hiding, and operating in fear, as Jacob did. Stop wandering in a spiritual wilderness.

Begin to function under the mantle of these tremendous promises. Like Jacob, you are already an heir of the covenant promises of God. Start acting like it. Start living like it.

CHAPTER SIX

BLESSED TO BE A BLESSING

We have been on a powerful, spiritual journey in this study. We have learned that God made an eternal, unchanging covenant with Abraham, which has continually extended through the centuries to us today. We have explored its many provisions and learned how we may enter into it.

One question remains: Why did God give us these tremendous blessings?

One reason, of course, is that God gave these promises to us because He loves us. He gave us these blessings in the same way that any good earthly father would pass an inheritance to his sons and daughters.

Jesus declared: *The thief cometh not, but for to steal, and to kill, and to destroy: I am come that they might have life, and that they might have it more abundantly* (John 10:10). God wants you to have a rich, abundant life.

Every good thing that you have comes from God: *Every good gift and every perfect gift is from above, and cometh down from the Father of lights, with whom is no variableness, neither shadow of turning* (James 1:17).

There is a much larger purpose than simply enjoying these blessings. The divine purpose is clear: God blessed Abraham so that through him, the nations of the world would be blessed.

God extended the provisions of this powerful covenant through the centuries to you and me so that we would be empowered to fulfill the Great Commission:

> *Go ye therefore, and teach all nations, baptizing them in the name of the Father, and of the Son, and of the Holy Ghost: Teaching them to observe all things whatsoever I have commanded you: and, lo, I am with you alway, even unto the end of the world. Amen.*
>
> Matthew 28:19-20

Why, through these promises, does God pledge supernatural success? Why does He promise all good things? Why does He declare that He will be our shield and bring wealth into our hands? Why does God want to bless us so much?

The reason is that there is a supernatural, spiritual harvest that is waiting to be reaped. It is unlike anything that we have ever witnessed. The Abrahamic blessing is a no-lack blessing that is promised by God. He declared that we would have sufficiency in all things:

> *And God is able to make all grace abound toward you; that ye, always having all sufficiency in all things, may abound to every good work:*
>
> II Corinthians 9:8

All sufficiency means everything we need to get the job done. This divine sufficiency is ours through the promises of Abraham. God wants to pour His blessings through you to the world. Paul told the Corinthians:

Chapter Six: Blessed To Be A Blessing

Not that we are sufficient of ourselves to claim anything as coming from us; our sufficiency is from God, who has qualified us to be ministers of a new covenant, not in a written code but in the Spirit; for the written code kills, but the Spirit gives life.

2 Corinthians 3:5-6, RSV

God has blessed you with the provisions of the Abrahamic Covenant so that you will be able to share with others as a minister of the new covenant. You will not minister in legalism and the letter of the law, but you will minister in the life of the Spirit because you are under the anointing of this powerful covenant.

To reap this mighty, spiritual harvest around the world and reach the nations with the good news of the gospel, we must have the power of these covenant promises behind us. God is opening new, strategic doors to spread the gospel. In order to respond, walk through these doors, and reap this great spiritual harvest, we must function under the power and provisions of the Abrahamic Covenant.

God has blessed you so that you can be a blessing:

- to your family.
- to your friends.
- to your community.
- to the nations of the world.

Believe and receive God's covenant promises. Make a demand on what is legally due to you, and claim it. As you appropriate these covenant promises, not only will all of your needs be met, but you will go forward — in a mighty demonstration of the miracle-working power of God — to accomplish the work that He has given you to accomplish for reaping the end-time harvest.

No matter what your past has been like or how troubled the future may seem in the natural, this is a new day for you spiritually. This is a day of the covenant promises of God being fulfilled in your life.

As Abraham, by faith, step out today, and embrace your divine destiny. Do what God said: *Ask of me, and I shall give thee the heathen for thine inheritance, and the uttermost parts of the earth for thy possession* (Psalms 2:8).

APPENDIX

PERSONALIZED DECLARATIONS OF THE ABRAHAMIC COVENANT

Use the following personalized declarations to claim the tremendous promises that are yours through the Abrahamic Covenant.

Genesis 12:1-3,7:

1. I will show thee a land and give it to thee (vv. 1,7).

   Make this declaration: *God will reveal my spiritual destiny.*

2. I will make of thee a great nation (v. 2).

   Make this declaration: *God will make my spiritual descendants great.*

3. I will bless thee (v. 2).

   Make this declaration: *God will bless me.*

4. I will make thy name great (v. 2).

   Make this declaration: *He will make my name great, of a good reputation.*

5. Thou shalt be a blessing (v. 2).

   Make this declaration: *He will make me a blessing.*

6. I will bless them that bless thee (v. 3).

   Make this declaration: *He will bless those that bless me.*

7. I will curse them that curse thee (v. 3).

   Make this declaration: *He will curse those who curse me.*

8. In thee shall all families of the earth be blessed (v. 3).

    Make this declaration: *The families (nations) of the earth will be blessed through me.*

Genesis 13:15-17:

9. All the land which thou seest, to thee will I give it forever (v. 15).

    Make this declaration: *All that God reveals to me is mine.*

10. I will also give the land to thy seed forever (v. 15).

    Make this declaration: *These blessings will extend to my spiritual seed.*

11. I will make thy seed as the dust of the earth (v. 16).

    Make this declaration: *My spiritual seed will be as the dust of the earth.*

12. Walk through the land, for I will give it unto thee (v. 17).

    Make this declaration: *Wherever God leads me, that spiritual territory is mine.*

Genesis 15:1-21:

13. I am thy shield (v. 1).

    Make this declaration: *God is my shield.*

14. I am thy exceeding great reward (v. 1).

    Make this declaration: *God is my exceeding great reward.*

15. He that shall come forth out of thine own loins shall be thine heir (v. 4).

    Make this declaration: *I will bring forth spiritual heirs.*

16. Abraham believed the Lord, and it was counted to him for righteousness (v. 6).

    Make this declaration: *I believe the Lord, and it is counted to me for righteousness.*

APPENDIX

17. Thy seed shall be as the stars of heaven (v. 5).

    Make this declaration: *My spiritual seed shall be as the stars of heaven.*

18. I am the Lord Who brought thee out of Ur of the Chaldees to give thee this land to inherit it (v. 7).

    Make this declaration: *God brought me out of the past to bring me into my spiritual inheritance.*

19. Thy seed shall be in bondage (slavery in Egypt) for 400 years (v. 13).

    Make this declaration: *God brought me out of the bondage of slavery to sin.*

20. The nation whom they shall serve (Egypt) will I judge (v. 14).

    Make this declaration: *God will judge those who enslaved me.*

21. Afterward, I will bring them out (of Egypt) with great substance (v. 14).

    Make this declaration: *I will be brought out of every bondage with great spiritual and material substance.*

22. Thou shalt go to thy fathers in peace (v. 15).

    Make this declaration: *I will join my godly ancestors in eternity.*

23. Thou shalt be buried in a good old age (v. 15).

    Make this declaration: *I will live to accomplish my destiny.*

24. In the fourth generation, thy seed shall come here again (v. 16).

    Make this declaration: *My seed will be preserved and return to their spiritual roots.*

25. Unto thy seed have I given this land (v. 18).

    Make this declaration: *My seed will inherit their rightful possessions.*

26. I will set the river of Egypt and the great Euphrates river as the boundaries of the Promised Land (v.18).

    Make this declaration: *God has established my spiritual boundaries, and nothing can change them.*

Genesis 17:1-22:

27. I will make my covenant between me and thee (Abraham) (v. 2).

    Make this declaration: *This is a supernatural covenant that has been established between God and me.*

28. I will multiply thee exceedingly (v. 2).

    Make this declaration: *God will multiply me exceedingly.*

29. My covenant is with thee (v. 4)

    Make this declaration: *God's covenant is with me.*

30. Thou shalt be a father of many nations (v. 4).

    Make this declaration: *I will be the spiritual parent of nations.*

31. Thy name shall be called Abraham rather than Abram (v. 5).

    Make this declaration: *God will change my spiritual identity to reflect His purposes.*

32. I will make thee exceedingly fruitful (v. 6).

    Make this declaration: *I will be exceedingly fruitful in every area of my life.*

33. I will make nations of thee (v. 6).

    Make this declaration: *I will be multiplied spiritually and affect the destiny of entire nations.*

34. Kings shall come out of thee (v. 6).

    Make this declaration: *I will raise up spiritually great men and women.*

APPENDIX

35. The covenant is everlasting (v. 7).

    Make this declaration: *This covenant is everlasting.*

36. I will be a God unto thee (v. 7).

    Make this declaration: *God will be God to me.*

37. I will be a God unto thy seed after thee (v. 7).

    Make this declaration: *He will be God to my spiritual and material seed.*

38. I will give all of the land of Canaan to you and to your seed as an everlasting possession (v. 8).

    Make this declaration: *God will give me my rightful inheritance as an everlasting possession.*

39. And I will be thy seed's God (v. 8).

    Make this declaration: *He will be the God of my children and grandchildren and for every generation to come.*

40. Circumcision sealed the covenant (vv. 9-14).

    Make this declaration: *This covenant has been sealed by the blood of Jesus Christ.*

41. Sarai's name shall be changed to Sarah (v. 15).

    Make this declaration: *Like Sarah, my spiritual identity will be changed, and I will become fruitful.*

42. I will bless Sarah (v. 16).

    Make this declaration: *God will bless me.*

43. I will give thee a son of Sarah (v. 16).

    Make this declaration: *God will raise up spiritual sons and daughters to me.*

44. Sarah will be a mother of nations (v. 16).

    Make this declaration: *I will be the spiritual mentor of nations.*

45. Kings of people shall be of Sarah (v. 16).

Make this declaration: *I will bring forth strong spiritual leaders.*

46. Sarah's son shall be named Isaac (v. 19).

Make this declaration: *My children will be birthed by the Spirit (like Isaac), not by the flesh (like Ishmael).*

47. I will establish My covenant with Isaac for an everlasting covenant (v. 19).

Make this declaration: *This covenant is established with me forever.*

48. I will establish My covenant with Isaac's seed after him for an everlasting covenant (v. 19).

Make this declaration: *This covenant is established with my seed forever.*

49. I will make Ishmael fruitful (v. 20).

Make this declaration: *God will make all who are related to me spiritually fruitful.*

50. I will multiply Ishmael exceedingly (v. 20).

Make this declaration: *God will multiply all who are related to me spiritually.*

51. Twelve princes shall Ishmael beget (v. 20).

Make this declaration: *I will bring forth spiritual heirs.*

52. I will make Ishmael a great nation (v. 20).

Make this declaration: *My seed will be a great spiritual nation.*

53. My covenant will I establish with Isaac, but I have blessed Ishmael also (vv. 20-21).

Make this declaration: *God will bless all of my efforts* (Ishmael), *but His divine covenant comes supernaturally through His Spirit* (Isaac).

APPENDIX

Genesis 22:16-18:

54. The covenant is guaranteed by God's oath (v. 16).

    Make this declaration: *God has guaranteed that these blessings are mine with His own oath.*

55. In blessing I will bless thee (v. 17).

    Make this declaration: *God will bless me as I bless others.*

56. In multiplying, I will multiply thy seed as the stars of the heaven and as the sand which is upon the sea shore (v. 17).

    Make this declaration: *God will multiply my spiritual seed as the stars and sand.*

57. Thy seed shall possess the gate of his enemies (v. 17).

    Make this declaration: *My spiritual seed will possess the gates of the enemy.*

58. In thy seed shall all families of the earth be blessed (v. 18).

    Make this declaration: *My spiritual seed will bless all families (the nations) of the earth.*

POSSESSING THE PROMISES: Claiming The Abrahamic Covenant

MY NEED
Record your personal need.

_____

_____

_____

_____

_____

_____

PROMISE OF ABRAHAM TO CLAIM
Record the reference for the promise of Abraham that is applicable to your personal need.

_____

_____

_____

_____

_____

HOW GOD MANIFESTED THIS PROMISE IN MY LIFE
Record how God met your need.

_____

_____

_____

_____

_____

POSSESSING THE PROMISES: Claiming The Abrahamic Covenant

MY NEED
Record your personal need.

_____
_____
_____
_____
_____
_____

PROMISE OF ABRAHAM TO CLAIM
Record the reference for the promise of Abraham that is applicable to your personal need.

_____
_____
_____
_____
_____
_____

HOW GOD MANIFESTED THIS PROMISE IN MY LIFE
Record how God met your need.

_____
_____
_____
_____
_____
_____

POSSESSING THE PROMISES: Claiming The Abrahamic Covenant

MY NEED
Record your personal need.

_____
_____
_____
_____
_____
_____

PROMISE OF ABRAHAM TO CLAIM
Record the reference for the promise of Abraham that is applicable to your personal need.

_____
_____
_____
_____
_____
_____

HOW GOD MANIFESTED THIS PROMISE IN MY LIFE
Record how God met your need.

_____
_____
_____
_____
_____
_____

POSSESSING THE PROMISES: Claiming The Abrahamic Covenant

MY NEED
Record your personal need.

_____
_____
_____
_____
_____
_____

PROMISE OF ABRAHAM TO CLAIM
Record the reference for the promise of Abraham that is applicable to your personal need.

_____
_____
_____
_____
_____
_____

HOW GOD MANIFESTED THIS PROMISE IN MY LIFE
Record how God met your need.

_____
_____
_____
_____
_____
_____

POSSESSING THE PROMISES: Claiming The Abrahamic Covenant

MY NEED
Record your personal need.

_____
_____
_____
_____
_____
_____
_____

PROMISE OF ABRAHAM TO CLAIM
Record the reference for the promise of Abraham that is applicable to your personal need.

_____
_____
_____
_____
_____
_____
_____

HOW GOD MANIFESTED THIS PROMISE IN MY LIFE
Record how God met your need.

_____
_____
_____
_____
_____
_____
_____

POSSESSING THE PROMISES: Claiming The Abrahamic Covenant

MY NEED
Record your personal need.

_____
_____
_____
_____
_____
_____

PROMISE OF ABRAHAM TO CLAIM
Record the reference for the promise of Abraham that is applicable to your personal need.

_____
_____
_____
_____
_____
_____

HOW GOD MANIFESTED THIS PROMISE IN MY LIFE
Record how God met your need.

_____
_____
_____
_____
_____
_____

POSSESSING THE PROMISES: Claiming The Abrahamic Covenant

MY NEED
Record your personal need.

PROMISE OF ABRAHAM TO CLAIM
Record the reference for the promise of Abraham that is applicable to your personal need.

HOW GOD MANIFESTED THIS PROMISE IN MY LIFE
Record how God met your need.

POSSESSING THE PROMISES: Claiming The Abrahamic Covenant

MY NEED
Record your personal need.

_____

_____

_____

_____

_____

_____

PROMISE OF ABRAHAM TO CLAIM
Record the reference for the promise of Abraham that is applicable to your personal need.

_____

_____

_____

_____

_____

_____

HOW GOD MANIFESTED THIS PROMISE IN MY LIFE
Record how God met your need.

_____

_____

_____

_____

_____

_____

POSSESSING THE PROMISES: Claiming The Abrahamic Covenant

MY NEED
Record your personal need.

PROMISE OF ABRAHAM TO CLAIM
Record the reference for the promise of Abraham that is applicable to your personal need.

HOW GOD MANIFESTED THIS PROMISE IN MY LIFE
Record how God met your need.

Brother Cerullo,

Please place these requests on the Miracle Prayer Altar, and pray for these needs:

_____
_____
_____
_____
_____

☐ Enclosed is my love gift of $(£)_____ to help you to win souls and to support this worldwide ministry.

☐ Please tell me how I can become a God's Victorious Army member to help you to reach the nations of the world, and receive even more anointed teachings on a monthly basis!

Name: _____
Address: _____
City: _____ State or Province: _____
Postal Code: _____ Phone: (___) _____
E-Mail: _____
Fax: _____

Mail today to:

MORRIS CERULLO WORLD EVANGELISM

San Diego: P.O. Box 85277, San Diego, CA 92186
Canada: P.O. Box 3600, Concord, Ontario L4K 1B6
U.K.: P.O. Box 277, Hemel Hempstead, Herts HP2 7DH

Web site: www.mcwe.com • E-Mail: morriscerullo@mcwe.com
For prayer 24 hours a day, 7 days a week, call: 1-858-HELPLINE
435-7546

HELPLINE FAX: (858) 427-0555
HELPLINE EMAIL: helpline@mcwe.com

OTHER BOOKS BY MORRIS CERULLO:
(not an exhaustive list)

Order your copy today by placing a check mark next to the book you want. See the reverse side for additional order information.

- ☐ *You Can Know How To Defeat Satan* — $15.00
- ☐ *Knowing God's Will For Your Life* — $10.00
- ☐ *God's Answers To Heal Your Deep Hurts* — $10.00
- ☐ *Why Do The Righteous Suffer?* — $8.00
- ☐ *How To Take The Limits Off God* — $8.00
- ☐ *Making Possible Your Impossibilities* — $5.00
- ☐ *How To Have The Power Of God* — $5.00
- ☐ *How To Break Satan's Cycle Of Defeat* — $5.00
- ☐ *God Has A Plan For Your Life* — $1.00

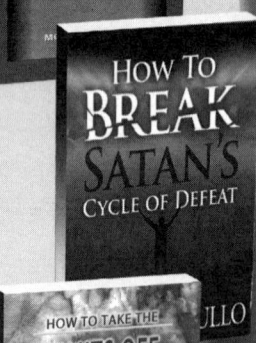